MAXIMIZING HUMAN PERFORMANCE IN SALES

Unlocking Your Best Results By Thinking Like A Business Owner

By Mort Greenberg

———————

To every salesperson for taking on the ultimate business challenge and navigating the road less traveled.

To all co-workers that have taken time to push me further and further to become a better business person and challenge me on everything, all of the time.

This book is dedicated to each you!

First Paperback edition January 2025

Print Paperback ISBN: 978-1-961059-10-8
Kindle KPF ISBN: 978-1-961059-11-5
Ingram EPUB ISBN: 978-1-961059-12-2

Published by digitalCORE www.dgtlcore.com

digitalCORE

Other Books by Mort Greenberg

REVENUE VS. SALES SERIES

- **The Singular Focus**
  100+ Tips to Maximize Your Revenue

- **Revenue Boost**
  The Ultimate Sales Plan in Five Steps

- **Straight Up Selling**
  Your Toolbox for Sales Excellence

THE FOCUSED SELLER SERIES

* **Maximizing Human Performance in Sales**

  Unlocking Your Best Results By Thinking Like A Business Owner

- **The Sales Tactician**
  Spycraft Techniques for Revenue Success

- **Elevate**
  Mastering the Art of Sales Leadership

- **Beyond The Acquisition**
  Thriving With Private Equity Ownership

CHILDREN'S BOOK SERIES

The Fearless Girl and The Little Guy with Greatness

- **Book 1** - Live Life Motivated
- **Book 2** - Young Leaders Guide
- **Book 3** - Asking Awesome Questions
- **Book 4** - Think to Win
- **Book 5** - Smart Money Moves
- **Book 6** - Wellness Warriors
- **Book 7** - Travel Like a Pro
- **Book 8** - Outdoor Skills

INTRODUCTION

Welcome to *"Maximizing Human Performance In Sales,"* the first volume in the "The Focused Seller" series. This book is your gateway to unlocking the full potential of your sales career by adopting the strategic mindset of a business owner. Here, we explore the essential skills and principles that pave the way for exceptional sales achievements and set the foundation for the advanced strategies detailed in the subsequent books.

In this initial volume, you will learn how to enhance your individual performance by integrating key business concepts into your daily sales practices. From mastering the art of negotiation and persuasion to effectively using technology to supercharge your results, this book provides the tools you need to operate at the highest level. You'll discover how to create sustainable success by building routines that optimize energy and productivity, all while maintaining genuine and impactful client relationships.

As you progress through the series, each book builds on the previous one, enhancing your skills and deepening your knowledge. After laying the groundwork here, you will move to *"The Sales Tactician: Spycraft Techniques for Revenue Success,"* where you'll learn to apply precision from the world of espionage to your sales techniques. Following that, *"Elevate: Mastering the Art of Sales Leadership"* will guide you through the nuances of sales leadership, empowering you to lead and inspire your team effectively. Finally, *"Beyond The Acquisition: Thriving with Private Equity Ownership"* offers insights into navigating the complexities and opportunities of private equity environments, ensuring you are equipped to handle strategic transitions and foster growth under new ownership.

"Maximizing Human Performance In Sales" is not just the starting point for your journey through "The Focused Seller" series; it is a crucial step towards becoming a top-tier professional in your

field. This book sets the stage for a comprehensive educational experience that will transform your approach to sales, leadership, and business management. Prepare to elevate your sales career to new heights, starting right here with the fundamental principles that every ambitious sales professional must know.

From the first page, this isn't just a book about selling; it's a book about becoming. It challenges you to think beyond quotas and transactions, urging you to adopt the mindset, strategies, and habits of top performers. Through its structure, it guides you to uncover the full potential of your own abilities while helping others do the same.

In my career, I've worked with some of the most exceptional sales professionals and business leaders from the early internet days to now. The one thing they all had in common wasn't just their talent; it was their commitment to learning, improving, and thinking strategically about their role in the bigger picture. The ideas presented in these chapters– treating your territory like your own business, mastering the art of storytelling, balancing work and life, and embracing leadership-are exactly what separates the extraordinary from the average.

This isn't a book you read once and set aside. It's a guide, a resource, and a call to action. Each chapter offers actionable insights and workshop activities that will challenge you to think critically and apply what you've learned immediately. Whether you're just starting out in sales or are a seasoned veteran looking to refine your craft, this book provides a roadmap to becoming a leader in your field.

As you turn these pages, remember that the journey of self-improvement in sales never ends. The lessons you'll find here are meant to inspire growth-not just in your career but in how you approach challenges, build relationships, and define success.

Author's Note

Sales has not only been the cornerstone of my career, but it's also been a lens through which I've come to view the world. Across roles at some of the world's most dynamic companies—Nokia, iHeart Media, NBC Universal, Ask Jeeves, and Excite.com—to founding FitAd, a first-of-its-kind digital fitness advertising platform, the lessons I've learned continue to push me harder to achieve more and more. These experiences shaped not just my approach to sales but my understanding of leadership, innovation, and human connection.

Throughout my journey, one principle has always stood out: success in sales isn't just about hitting quotas—it's about creating value. It's about forging genuine connections with people, understanding their challenges, and crafting solutions that truly make a difference. This philosophy has informed not only my career but also my writing, from my three book series Revenue vs. Sales to my eight-book children's series The Fearless Girl and the Little Guy with Greatness. Whether writing for business leaders or young dreamers, my goal has always been the same: to inspire, to empower, and to help others realize their potential.

Maximizing Human Performance in Sales is a culmination of decades of experience across industries and roles. It's a guide for sales professionals who want to go beyond transactions and truly master their craft. In these pages, you'll find actionable strategies for excelling in a rapidly changing world, from leveraging AI to building trust in an age of automation. You'll also find timeless lessons about resilience, empathy, and the enduring power of thinking like a business owner.

This book isn't just for sales professionals—it's for anyone looking to lead with purpose and drive meaningful impact. It's about building sustainable success, not just for yourself but for those around you. Whether you're closing a multimillion-dollar deal or mentoring a junior colleague, the principles here will help you achieve your goals while staying true to the human side of sales.

Sales has always been about people, and no amount of technology will ever replace the importance of trust, empathy, and collaboration. As you dive into this book, I encourage you to think beyond tactics and focus on building relationships that last—both with your clients and within your own life. Thank you for joining me on this journey. I hope this book inspires you, challenges you, and equips you to reach new heights. Here's to making every connection count and every sale a meaningful one.

Sincerely,
Mort Greenberg

Table of Contents

THE FOUNDATION OF SALES EXCELLENCE

This section lays the groundwork for what it takes to become a top-performing salesperson. It emphasizes the importance of developing the right mindset, understanding the science behind human performance, and mastering the fundamentals of economics in sales. Each chapter provides actionable insights into building mental resilience, optimizing physical and emotional energy, and thinking strategically about the financial principles that drive business decisions. By focusing on personal growth and foundational skills, this section prepares you to operate at your peak and navigate the complex dynamics of sales.

CHAPTER 1

The Salesperson's Mindset

> ❝
>
> *Success in sales starts with the right mindset—one that embraces growth, builds resilience, and turns challenges into opportunities.*
>
> ❞

Sales is a profession that demands both skill and stamina. It requires the courage to face rejection, the creativity to solve complex problems, and the drive to improve continuously. At the heart of it all lies the salesperson's mindset—a foundational element determining success or failure. This chapter explores developing a growth mindset, harnessing intrinsic motivation, and building resilience and adaptability to thrive in any sales environment.

Developing
a Growth Mindset

A growth mindset, a concept popularized by psychologist Carol Dweck, is the belief that abilities and intelligence can be developed through dedication and hard work. In sales, this mindset is essential for embracing challenges, learning from failures, and achieving consistent improvement.

Example:

Consider Sarah, a young sales representative at a tech startup. She struggled to close deals in her first six months and often doubted her abilities. Instead of giving up, she reframed her failures as learning opportunities. Sarah transformed her performance by seeking feedback from her manager, studying her competitors' approaches, and practicing her pitch daily. Within a year, she became the top salesperson in her region. Her success stemmed not from innate talent but from her commitment to growth.

Practical Tips for a Growth Mindset:

- **Seek Feedback Regularly:** Embrace constructive criticism as a tool for improvement.
- **Set Incremental Goals:** Break down large objectives into smaller, achievable tasks.
- **Celebrate Progress:** Recognize even small wins to stay motivated and confident.

Harnessing

Intrinsic Motivation

Intrinsic motivation is the internal drive to pursue goals for personal satisfaction rather than external rewards. It's what keeps top salespeople passionate and persistent, even in the face of challenges.

The Power of Purpose

Top-performing salespeople often align their work with a greater purpose. For instance, a healthcare salesperson might focus on how their products improve patient lives, finding deeper meaning in their role.

Example:

A senior account executive, Michael consistently exceeded his quotas not because of the commissions but because he genuinely enjoyed helping clients solve problems. He often reminded himself of his mission: to empower businesses with innovative solutions. This intrinsic motivation kept him energized and engaged, even during challenging periods.

Practical Tips for Intrinsic Motivation:

- **Identify Your "Why":** Write down why you chose sales as a profession.
- **Focus on Impact:** Consider how your work benefits clients and their organizations.
- **Find Joy in Mastery:** Take pride in improving your craft, regardless of external validation.

The Importance of Resilience and Adaptability

Resilience is the ability to bounce back from setbacks, while adaptability is the capacity to pivot strategies in response to changing circumstances. In sales, these traits are indispensable for handling rejection, market fluctuations, and evolving customer needs.

Example of Resilience:

Jessica, a real estate agent, lost three major deals in one month. Instead of dwelling on her losses, she analyzed what went wrong and adjusted her approach. She invested in training to improve her negotiation skills and rebuilt her pipeline with fresh leads. By the end of the quarter, she not only recovered but surpassed her previous performance.

Example of Adaptability:

During the pandemic, a B2B software company saw in-person meetings vanish overnight. Their sales team, led by an adaptable mindset, quickly transitioned to virtual demos and webinars.

They invested in digital tools and retrained on remote selling techniques, ensuring their success in a drastically changed landscape.

Practical Tips for Resilience and Adaptability:

- **Practice Emotional Agility:** Acknowledge setbacks without letting them define you.
- **Embrace Change:** View new challenges as opportunities to learn and innovate.
- **Stay Proactive:** Anticipate industry trends and adapt your strategies accordingly.

Workshop
Activities

To turn this chapter into an interactive learning experience, try the following activities:

1. Growth Mindset Reflection
- Write about a recent sales challenge you faced.
- Identify what you learned from the experience and how you can apply that knowledge moving forward.

2. Discover Your "Why"
- Take 15 minutes to reflect on why you chose sales as a profession.
- Write a paragraph describing the personal satisfaction you derive from helping clients. Share this with a partner or group.

3. Resilience Role-Play
- In pairs, role-play a difficult client rejection.
- Practice handling the rejection with composure and brainstorming a follow-up plan.

- Switch roles and provide constructive feedback to each other.

4. Adaptability Brainstorm
- Divide into small groups and discuss a major industry trend or challenge (e.g., AI in sales, economic downturns).
- Develop a sales strategy that embraces the change and present it to the group.

5. Personal Growth Plan
- Create a 30-day plan with one goal for improving your mindset, motivation, resilience, or adaptability.
- Identify specific actions you'll take and a method for tracking your progress.

Conclusion

The salesperson's mindset is not static; it's a dynamic force shaped by daily habits, perspectives, and decisions. By developing a growth mindset, harnessing intrinsic motivation, and cultivating resilience and adaptability, you lay the foundation for long-term success in sales. Remember, the most successful salespeople don't just work harder—they think and grow smarter. Now, it's your turn to build the mindset that will set you apart.

CHAPTER 2

The Science of Human Performance

> **"**
>
> *Peak sales performance comes from optimizing your body, mind, and emotions, because energy drives execution.*
>
> **"**

Sales is more than just skill and strategy—it's also about leveraging your physical, mental, and emotional energy to perform at your best consistently. This chapter explores the science behind optimizing human performance, how neuroscience informs decision-making in sales, and how to manage your time and energy cycles to maximize productivity. Understanding these principles can help you close more deals, build stronger relationships, and sustain long-term success.

Physical, Mental, and Emotional Optimization for Peak Sales Performance

Physical Optimization

Sales is a demanding career, often involving long hours, high-pressure situations, and constant travel. Physical health is foundational to sustaining energy and focus.

Example:

Consider James, a field sales executive who constantly felt drained during his afternoon calls. After consulting a health coach, he discovered his diet was full of processed sugars, leading to energy crashes. By switching to a protein-rich breakfast and incorporating regular exercise, James experienced increased stamina and sharper focus throughout the day.

Tips for Physical Optimization:

- **Sleep:** Prioritize 7–8 hours of quality sleep each night to boost focus and decision-making.
- **Nutrition:** Eat balanced meals with lean protein, whole grains, and vegetables to maintain energy.
- **Exercise:** Incorporate 30 minutes of physical activity daily to reduce stress and enhance mental clarity.

Mental Optimization

The ability to stay focused, process information, and think strategically is critical in sales. Mental optimization involves enhancing cognitive abilities through mindfulness and stress management.

Example:

Sophia, a B2B account manager, began meditating for 10 minutes each morning. Over time, she noticed improved concentration during lengthy negotiations and greater patience with difficult clients.

Tips for Mental Optimization:

- **Mindfulness:** Practice meditation or deep breathing exercises to reduce stress and improve focus.
- **Learning:** Dedicate time to learning new skills or industry knowledge to keep your mind sharp.
- **Avoid Multitasking:** Focus on one task at a time to improve efficiency and accuracy.

Emotional

Optimization

Sales success depends on managing emotions—both yours and your clients'. Emotional intelligence (EQ) includes self-awareness, empathy, and the ability to regulate emotions under pressure.

Example:

David, a sales representative, used to get frustrated when prospects hesitated. After attending an EQ workshop, he learned to recognize his triggers and approach objections with empathy. This shift led to more productive conversations and higher conversion rates.

Tips for Emotional Optimization:

- **Self-Awareness:** Regularly reflect on your emotional responses during interactions.
- **Empathy:** Try to understand the client's perspective fully before responding.
- **Emotional Regulation:** Use techniques like reframing negative thoughts to stay calm under pressure.

Neuroscience and
Decision-Making in Sales

The human brain is wired to make decisions based on both logic and emotion. Understanding these mechanisms can help salespeople influence prospects more effectively.

The Power of Emotional Triggers

People often make purchasing decisions based on emotions and then justify them with logic. Successful salespeople learn to appeal to both.

Example:

Emily, a SaaS salesperson, found that emphasizing how her software reduced stress for team managers resonated more than focusing solely on features. By addressing the emotional pain point first, she closed deals faster.

Neuroscience Principles for Sales:

- **Dopamine and Reward:** Frame your pitch to highlight benefits and positive outcomes, activating the client's reward system.
- **Fear and Loss Aversion:** Use urgency or scarcity to tap into the brain's natural aversion to loss (e.g., "This offer is available for a limited time").
- **Social Proof:** Share testimonials or case studies to build trust, leveraging the brain's preference for herd behavior.

Time Management
and Energy Cycles:
Selling at Your Peak Hours

Not all hours of the day are created equal. Understanding your natural energy cycles—often referred to as circadian rhythms—can help you schedule tasks for peak productivity.

Identifying Your Peak Hours
Everyone has specific times during the day when they feel most alert and focused. For many, this is mid-morning or early afternoon, but it varies by individual.

Example:

Carlos tracked his energy levels for a week and discovered his focus peaked between 9 a.m. and 11 a.m. He began scheduling his most important client calls during this window and reserved administrative tasks for the late afternoon when his energy dipped.

The Two-Hour Rule

Research shows that most people can focus intensely for about two hours before needing a break. Use this insight to structure your workday.

Example Schedule:

9:00–11:00	High-priority client calls or presentations.
11:00–11:30	Break or light administrative work.
13:00–15:00	Follow-ups, proposals, or strategic planning.
15:00–17:00	Emails, CRM updates, and lower-energy tasks.

Practical Tips for Time Management:

- **Batch Similar Tasks:** Group similar activities (e.g., prospecting calls) to maintain focus.
- **Take Breaks:** Use techniques like the Pomodoro Method (25 minutes of work, 5-minute break) to stay fresh.
- **Avoid Energy Drains:** Limit multitasking and minimize distractions, especially during peak hours.

Workshop
Activities

1. Energy Tracking Exercise
- Over the next week, record your energy levels at different times of the day.
- Identify your peak hours and plan your next sales day accordingly.

2. Mindfulness Practice
- Begin each day with a 5-minute breathing or meditation exercise.
- Write down how it affects your focus and stress levels after a week.

3. Emotional Trigger Mapping
- Choose three clients and analyze their emotional triggers.
- Develop a pitch that addresses both their emotional and logical needs.

4. Time Management Audit
- For one week, track how you spend each hour of your workday.
- Identify inefficiencies and create a revised schedule to maximize productivity.

5. Neuroscience Role-Play
- Pair up and practice using emotional triggers, social proof, and urgency in your sales pitch.
- Give feedback on how effectively the techniques influenced decision-making.

Conclusion

The science of human performance is the hidden advantage that separates good salespeople from great ones. By optimizing your physical, mental, and emotional state, leveraging neuroscience principles, and working in harmony with your energy cycles, you can consistently operate at your peak. Remember, the key to sustained success is not just working harder but working smarter—aligned with your body and mind's natural rhythms.

CHAPTER 3

The Economics of Sales

"

Understanding the economic forces behind every deal empowers you to align your solutions with what truly drives your client's decisions.

"

Sales isn't just about relationships and persuasion—it's deeply rooted in economics. Understanding basic economic principles, supply and demand dynamics, and pricing strategies equips salespeople with the knowledge to position their products effectively, negotiate confidently, and create value for their clients. This chapter explores these essential concepts and how they apply to real-world sales scenarios.

Basic Economic Principles Every Salesperson Should Know

1. Scarcity and Value

In economics, scarcity drives value. The rarer a product or service, the more valuable it becomes. Sales professionals must communicate scarcity—whether it's limited availability, exclusive features, or unique benefits—to enhance perceived value.

Example:

A luxury car salesperson emphasizes that only 500 units of a particular model are manufactured annually. This scarcity creates urgency and exclusivity, making the product more desirable.

2. Opportunity Cost

Opportunity cost is the value of the best alternative forgone when a choice is made. Clients often evaluate your product or service by comparing it to other options, including doing nothing.

Example:

A software salesperson illustrates how their product will save 10 hours per week for a client's team, showing the cost of continuing with their current inefficient system.

3. Marginal Utility

Marginal utility is the added satisfaction a customer receives from consuming one more unit of a product or service. In sales, understanding when a client has reached peak utility (or diminished returns) helps tailor pitches effectively.

Example:

A SaaS company offers tiered pricing based on features. By understanding when a client has maxed out the value of their current plan, the salesperson can suggest an upgrade to unlock new benefits.

Supply and Demand Dynamics
and Their Role in Sales

Supply and demand are the backbone of economic theory. These dynamics dictate market conditions and influence how salespeople position their products.

1. Demand: Understanding Client Needs

Demand represents the client's willingness and ability to buy a product. High demand often signals an opportunity to increase prices or upsell, while low demand may require additional incentives.

Example:

During the holiday season, e-commerce platforms

see high demand for tech gadgets. Sales reps use this demand to upsell extended warranties or accessories.

2. Supply: Managing Availability

Supply reflects how much of a product is available. Limited supply can create urgency, while oversupply may lead to discounts or added value offers.

Example:

A car dealership running low on electric vehicle inventory uses this scarcity to drive higher prices. Conversely, an overstocked SUV model prompts a promotion with zero-interest financing.

3. Equilibrium: Finding the Sweet Spot

The balance between supply and demand determines pricing. Salespeople must recognize when their product is in high demand but short supply to maximize profitability—or when to offer discounts to move excess inventory.

Example:

A luxury watch brand introduces a new collection in limited quantities, pricing it at a premium. As demand stabilizes, older models are discounted to clear inventory and make way for new designs.

Understanding Pricing Strategies and Market Positioning

Pricing strategies and positioning influence how a product is perceived and its success in the market.

1. Cost-Based Pricing

This strategy involves setting a price based on production costs plus a markup. While straightforward, it may not fully reflect the value to the client.

Example:

A furniture company calculates the cost of materials and labor at $200 and adds a 50% markup, selling the item for $300. While profitable, the pricing may not capture additional value perceived by high-end customers.

2. Value-Based Pricing

Value-based pricing aligns with the client's willingness to pay, focusing on the perceived benefits rather than the cost of production.

Example:

A cybersecurity firm prices its software at $50,000 annually, emphasizing the millions of dollars clients could save by preventing data breaches.

3. Competitive Pricing

This strategy considers competitor prices to position the product appropriately. It's effective in crowded markets but requires differentiation.

Example:

A new energy drink brand prices its product slightly below established competitors while highlighting unique ingredients to attract price-sensitive yet health-conscious consumers.

4. Dynamic Pricing

Dynamic pricing adjusts based on demand, time, or customer segments. This strategy is common in industries like travel, retail, and technology.

Example:

An airline charges higher fares during peak travel times and offers discounts during off-peak periods, maximizing revenue.

5. Market Positioning

Market positioning defines how a product is perceived relative to competitors. Effective positioning requires clear communication of unique selling points (USPs).

Example:

Tesla positions itself as a premium electric vehicle brand focused on innovation and sustainability, allowing it to command higher prices than most competitors.

Workshop

Activities

1. Opportunity Cost Exercise

- Identify three common objections clients have about your product (e.g., "It's too expensive").
- Write a counterargument for each, emphasizing the opportunity cost of not purchasing your product.

2. Supply and Demand Simulation

- In small groups, role-play a sales scenario where supply is either high or low, and demand fluctuates.
- Practice adjusting your pitch and pricing strategy based on the scenario.

3. Pricing Strategy Brainstorm

- Choose a product or service you sell and analyze which pricing strategy fits best: cost-based, value-based, competitive, or dynamic.
- Discuss how to position your product effectively using this strategy.

4. Market Positioning Map

- Create a positioning map comparing your product to two main competitors based on price and perceived value.
- Identify ways to differentiate your product and communicate its unique value.

5. Case Study: Price Elasticity

- Analyze a real-world case where a product's price increase or decrease significantly impacted demand.
- Discuss what sales strategies could have supported the pricing decision.

Conclusion

Sales and economics are deeply intertwined. By understanding basic principles like scarcity, opportunity cost, and marginal utility, and leveraging supply-demand dynamics, salespeople can position their products effectively and drive better outcomes. Pricing strategies and market positioning further empower you to maximize profitability while delivering value to clients. Mastering these economic fundamentals will not only make you a better salesperson but also a strategic partner for your clients. Now, let's put these principles into action.

UNDERSTANDING BUSINESS OPERATIONS

In Section 2, we shift the focus from individual performance to understanding the inner workings of businesses. These chapters explore how key operational functions—like marketing, finance, and supply chain management—interact and how sales professionals can align their strategies to complement these areas. You'll also learn how to think like a business owner, seeing the bigger picture of how your solutions impact clients' goals. With deep dives into industry-specific challenges and strategies for aligning with operational priorities, this section equips you to speak the language of decision-makers and position yourself as a trusted advisor.

CHAPTER 4

Thinking Like a Business Owner

> **"**
>
> *The best salespeople think like business owners—focusing on the big picture and aligning their efforts with their clients' goals.*
>
> **"**

The best salespeople don't just think like sales professionals; they think like business owners. They understand their clients' challenges, financial priorities, and strategic goals. By learning to see the big picture, grasping financial fundamentals, and connecting their product or service to the client's return on investment (ROI), salespeople can elevate their role from vendor to trusted advisor. This chapter explores these principles and provides actionable steps to adopt an owner's mindset.

Learning to See
the Big Picture

Thinking like a business owner requires stepping back from the transactional nature of sales and considering the broader context of the client's business. This means understanding how your product or service fits into their goals, challenges, and industry trends.

Key Areas to Focus On:

1. Client's Strategic Objectives: What are the company's short- and long-term goals? For example, are they trying to increase market share, reduce costs, or innovate?

2. Industry Dynamics: What trends or challenges are shaping their industry?

3. Decision-Making Process: Who are the key stakeholders, and how do they evaluate potential purchases?

Example:

A salesperson for an industrial machinery company noticed that their client was expanding operations into renewable energy. By researching this shift, they proposed a solution tailored to the client's sustainability goals, positioning themselves as a strategic partner rather than just a supplier.

Practical Steps to See the Big Picture:

- Research your client's industry and competitors before every meeting.

- Ask open-ended questions to uncover their strategic priorities.
- Monitor economic trends that could impact their business, such as interest rates or supply chain disruptions.

Profit and Loss: What Every Salesperson Must Understand About Financial Statements

Business owners live and breathe their financials. Salespeople who understand these concepts can better align their pitch with the client's priorities.

1. Key Financial Statements

- **Profit and Loss Statement (P&L):** Shows the company's revenues, costs, and profits over a specific period. Salespeople should focus on how their solution impacts the client's revenues (top line) or costs (bottom line).
- **Balance Sheet:** Highlights the company's assets, liabilities, and equity. Knowing a client's financial position can reveal their investment capacity.
- **Cash Flow Statement:** Indicates the inflow and outflow of cash. A product that improves cash flow—such as one that accelerates payments or reduces upfront costs—can be particularly appealing.

> **Example:**
> A SaaS salesperson pitching accounting software to a mid-sized company focused on how the solution

would automate processes, saving $50,000 annually in labor costs and improving cash flow by speeding up accounts receivable collections.

Key Metrics to Know:

- **Gross Margin:** The percentage of revenue remaining after direct costs (e.g., "Our product will improve your gross margin by reducing production costs").
- **Operating Expenses:** Fixed and variable costs (e.g., "This service will lower your marketing spend while increasing conversions").
- **Net Profit:** The company's bottom line, where sales can make a direct impact.

The Connection Between Your Product/Service and the Customer's ROI

Return on Investment (ROI) is the gold standard for justifying any business expense. Salespeople must articulate how their solution provides measurable value, whether through cost savings, revenue growth, or intangible benefits like brand equity.

Calculating ROI:

ROI is typically expressed as a percentage:

$$ROI = \frac{Net\ Gain\ from\ Investment - Cost\ of\ Investment}{Cost\ of\ Investment} \times 100$$

Example:

You sell a software solution for **$10,000** anually. The client will save **$50,000** in labor cost and increase revenues by **$20,000**

$$ROI = \frac{(50{,}000 + 20{,}000) - 10{,}000}{10{,}000} \; x \; 100 = \textbf{600\%}$$

Articulating this ROI in conversations makes the value proposition compelling and clear.

ROI Beyond Dollars:

Not all ROI is financial. Many clients value time savings, risk reduction, or employee satisfaction. For example, a healthcare company might value a solution that ensures compliance with regulations even if the financial ROI is modest.

Example:

A project management tool salesperson demonstrates how their software reduces project completion times by 20%, which translates to faster product launches and improved competitiveness for their client.

1. Big Picture Analysis

- Research a fictional or real company in your industry.
- Identify its strategic priorities, industry challenges, and decision-making process.
- Present a sales strategy tailored to this company's big-picture goals.

2. Financial Statement Exercise

- Provide a sample P&L statement for a fictional client.
- Ask participants to identify where their product or service could reduce costs or increase revenues.

3. ROI Calculation Practice

- Create a scenario where participants calculate ROI for a given product or service.
- Discuss how to communicate the results effectively to a client.

4. Role-Playing: Aligning with Owner's Mindset

- One participant acts as a business owner, sharing their company's goals and challenges.
- Another participant acts as the salesperson, tailoring their pitch to align with those priorities.
- Provide feedback on how well they addressed financial and strategic concerns.

5. Connecting to Non-Financial ROI

- Split into groups and brainstorm non-financial benefits your product offers (e.g., time savings, risk reduction, employee satisfaction).
- Develop a narrative to present these benefits compellingly to a client.

Conclusion

Thinking like a business owner is about more than just closing deals—it's about creating value. By learning to see the big picture, understanding the client's financial priorities, and articulating the connection between your product and their ROI, you position yourself as a true partner in their success. With these tools and insights, you'll not only sell more effectively but also foster deeper, longer-lasting relationships with your clients.

CHAPTER 5

The Inner Workings of a Business

> **"**
>
> *To sell effectively, you must understand how a client's business operates, from marketing and finance to supply chains and beyond.*
>
> **"**

To sell effectively, sales professionals need more than just product knowledge and charisma—they must understand the inner workings of their clients' businesses. This means grasping key operational functions like marketing, finance, and supply chain management, and learning to align sales strategies with the buyer's operational goals. By delving into these areas and industry-specific challenges, salespeople can position themselves as invaluable problem solvers and strategic partners.

Key Operational Functions: Marketing, Finance, and Supply Chain Management

1. Marketing: The Voice of the Customer

Marketing is the function that identifies customer needs, creates demand, and shapes the company's public image. A successful salesperson should understand the interplay between sales and marketing.

Key Insights for Salespeople:

- Marketing creates leads and brand awareness, which sales convert into revenue.
- Sales feedback can help marketing refine campaigns to better align with customer needs.
- Marketing budgets are often tied to ROI, so pitches that support measurable outcomes (e.g., higher lead conversions) resonate well.

Example:

A sales rep for a social media analytics tool learns that their client's marketing team struggles to measure campaign effectiveness. The rep tailors the pitch to highlight how the tool provides real-time metrics, enabling data-driven marketing decisions.

2. Finance: The Lifeblood of the Business

Finance oversees budgeting, forecasting, and resource allocation. Understanding the financial lens helps salespeople justify their product as a valuable investment.

Key Insights for Salespeople:

- Finance teams evaluate purchases based on ROI, payback periods, and cost reductions.
- Budgets are not just limits but strategic priorities; aligning your pitch with these priorities shows you understand the client's constraints.

Example:

A SaaS vendor presenting to a CFO emphasizes how their software can reduce operating costs by 15%, aligning with the company's goal of improving profitability by year-end.

3. Supply Chain Management: The Backbone of Operations

Supply chain management ensures that goods and services are delivered efficiently and cost-effectively. Salespeople working with logistics, manufacturing, or retail clients should understand this function deeply.

Key Insights for Salespeople:

Supply chain optimization revolves around reducing costs, improving speed, and maintaining quality. Any disruption in the supply chain can significantly impact revenue, making risk-reduction solutions highly appealing.

Aligning Your Pitch with the Buyer's Operational Goals

When crafting a pitch, salespeople must align their solution with the specific operational goals of their buyer. These goals often revolve around efficiency, cost reduction, risk mitigation, or growth.

Steps to Align Your Pitch:

1. Research the Client's Priorities: Use public reports, press releases, or direct conversations to identify key operational goals.
2. Speak Their Language: Use industry-specific terminology to demonstrate your understanding of their business.
3. Show Direct Impact: Quantify how your product or service addresses their operational needs.

Understanding Industry-Specific Business Challenges

Every industry faces unique challenges. Salespeople who understand these intricacies can build stronger relationships and deliver more relevant solutions.

Examples of Industry Challenges:

- **Healthcare:** Regulatory compliance, patient outcomes, and cost containment.
- **Retail:** Inventory management, e-commerce competition, and customer loyalty.
- **Tech:** Talent retention, rapid innovation cycles, and cybersecurity.
- **Manufacturing:** Rising raw material costs, supply chain disruptions, and sustainability pressures.

Example:

A sales rep targeting the retail industry highlights how their solution reduces inventory errors by 30%, addressing a common pain point for large retailers managing thousands of SKUs.

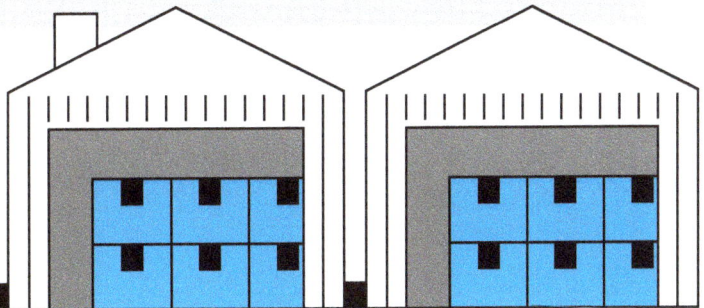

Workshop

Activities

1. Operational Goals Mapping

- Select a client or industry of interest.
- Research and list three key operational goals for that client or industry.
- Develop a tailored pitch that addresses one of these goals.

2. Marketing-Driven Pitch Practice

- Role-play as a marketing director presenting your operational challenges to a salesperson.
- Practice tailoring your pitch to show how your solution supports measurable marketing objectives, like increasing lead conversion rates.

3. Finance-Focused ROI Exercise

- Provide a sample scenario (e.g., a company considering a $50,000 investment).
- Ask participants to calculate the ROI of their solution and explain it in terms a CFO would value.

4. Supply Chain Challenge Simulation

- Create a scenario where a company faces a specific supply chain challenge (e.g., delayed shipments).
- Ask participants to propose a solution and articulate how it reduces risks or improves efficiency.

5. Industry Challenge Brainstorm

- Divide into groups, assigning each group a different industry.
- Have each group identify three key challenges in their assigned industry and
- brainstorm how their product or service could address them.

Conclusion

Understanding the inner workings of a business—its key functions, operational goals, and industry-specific challenges—empowers salespeople to craft pitches that resonate on a strategic level. By aligning your solutions with the needs of marketing, finance, or supply chain teams, you position yourself as a valuable partner in your client's success. Mastering this approach will not only elevate your sales results but also build lasting relationships founded on trust and mutual understanding. Now, let's put this knowledge into action!

CHAPTER 6

Strategic Selling

"

Strategic selling isn't just about closing deals—it's about aligning short-term wins with long-term client value.

"

Strategic selling goes beyond product knowledge and persuasion—it involves understanding your client's business goals and crafting tailored solutions that deliver value. To succeed, sales professionals must master crafting value-based propositions, speaking the language of C-suite executives, and balancing short-term wins with long-term value. This chapter will explore these essential elements and how to implement them effectively in your sales approach.

Crafting Value-Based Propositions

A value-based proposition focuses on how your product or service solves a client's problem or delivers measurable benefits. Instead of emphasizing features, you highlight the specific outcomes the client will achieve.

Steps to Craft a Value-Based Proposition:

1. Understand the Client's Pain Points:
Identify their challenges or unmet needs through research and discovery questions.

2. Link Features to Benefits:
Translate the features of your product into tangible benefits that address the client's needs.

3. Quantify the Impact:
Use data to show how your solution creates measurable results, such as increased revenue, cost savings, or improved efficiency.

Example:
A CRM software salesperson learns that their client struggles with inefficient lead tracking. Instead of emphasizing the software's technical features, they present a value proposition: "Our CRM reduces manual data entry by 70%, giving your sales team an additional 10 hours per week to focus on closing deals, which could increase revenue by 20% within six months."

Speaking the Language of C-Suite Executives

C-suite executives (CEOs, CFOs, COOs, etc.) think in terms of strategy, ROI, and risk management. To win their trust, you must align your message with their priorities.

How to Speak Their Language:

1. Focus on Business Outcomes:
Avoid getting bogged down in technical details; instead, highlight the strategic benefits of your solution.

2. Use Financial Metrics:
Speak in terms of ROI, cost reduction, revenue growth, or other financial impacts that resonate with executives.

3. Show Industry Expertise:
Demonstrate an understanding of their business and industry challenges, positioning yourself as a knowledgeable advisor.

Example:
A cybersecurity vendor meeting with a CFO focuses on how their solution reduces the financial risk of data breaches (estimated at $4.5 million per incident) while aligning with regulatory compliance requirements. They emphasize how this minimizes liability and protects the company's reputation.

Tailoring Solutions for Short-Term Wins and Long-Term Value

Clients often have immediate needs but also aim to achieve sustainable growth. A strategic salesperson addresses both by balancing quick wins with lasting value.

Short-Term Wins:

These are immediate results that demonstrate the effectiveness of your solution and build trust with the client.

Example:

A logistics company offers a 3-month trial of their route optimization software, showing a 15% reduction in fuel costs within the first month.

Long-Term Value:

This involves positioning your product as a strategic investment that supports the client's future goals.

Example:

The same logistics company highlights how the software integrates with their long-term sustainability goals, reducing the company's carbon footprint over five years.

Crafting Dual-Focused Solutions:

1. Address Urgent Needs:
Identify quick wins to solve pressing problems.

2. Show Strategic Alignment:
Connect your solution to the client's broader objectives, such as market expansion or operational efficiency.

3. Build Flexibility:
Offer scalable solutions that adapt as the client's business grows.

Examples of Strategic
Selling in Action

1. Healthcare SaaS Solution:

- **Client Need:** A hospital wants to reduce patient wait times (short-term) while improving overall care quality (long-term).

- **Sales Approach:** Highlight how the SaaS platform reduces wait times by automating scheduling, and emphasize long-term benefits like better patient outcomes and increased satisfaction scores.

2. Retail E-Commerce Platform:

- **Client Need:** A retailer seeks to improve holiday season sales (short-term) while building brand loyalty (long-term).

- **Sales Approach:** Focus on how the platform optimizes product recommendations for holiday shoppers, leading to a 25% sales boost, while fostering personalized shopping experiences that improve customer retention.

1. Crafting a Value-Based Proposition

- Select a product or service you sell.
- Identify a common client pain point and craft a value-based proposition using the following structure:
  - ◼ Pain Point
  - ◼ Feature
  - ◼ Benefit
  - ◼ Quantifiable Outcome
- Present your proposition to a partner for feedback.

2. C-Suite Role-Play

- One participant acts as a C-suite executive (CEO, CFO, or COO) with specific goals (e.g., reducing costs, increasing market share).
- The salesperson must pitch their solution using financial metrics and strategic language.
- Rotate roles and provide constructive feedback.

3. Short-Term and Long-Term Pitch Development

- Choose a real or fictional client.
- Develop a pitch that addresses both short-term wins and long-term value.
- Share your pitch with the group and discuss how well it balances immediate and strategic goals.

4. Executive Summary Exercise

- Write a one-page executive summary for a product

or service you sell.
- Focus on the strategic value, financial impact, and industry relevance of your solution.
- Use this summary to present your pitch concisely in a mock meeting.

5. Strategic Sales Problem-Solving
- Divide into groups and provide a case study of a business facing specific challenges.
- Each group crafts a tailored solution that addresses both the client's immediate needs and long-term objectives.
- Present solutions to the group and discuss their effectiveness.

Conclusion

Strategic selling is the art of aligning your pitch with the client's business goals, speaking in terms that resonate with decision-makers, and delivering both short-term results and long-term value. By mastering these skills, you elevate your role from salesperson to trusted partner, driving not only deals but also meaningful client relationships. Strategic selling is about seeing the bigger picture, thinking ahead, and always keeping the client's success at the forefront of your approach. Now, let's put these principles into practice!

BECOMING AN OWNER-MINDED SALESPERSON

Section 3 ties together the skills and knowledge from the earlier sections to focus on executing strategic sales techniques. You'll explore the nuances of crafting value-based propositions, building trust through empathy and insight, and differentiating yourself in a crowded market. This section also emphasizes the importance of taking ownership in the sales process—treating your territory like a business, balancing risk-taking with calculated decisions, and learning from setbacks to iterate and grow. By mastering these skills, you'll become not just a salesperson but a strategic partner who delivers lasting value for clients and achieves consistent success.

CHAPTER 7

Empathy and Insight

> *The best salespeople listen deeply, uncover hidden needs, and build trust through empathy and actionable insight.*

In the world of sales, the ability to understand and connect with clients is as critical as product knowledge or closing techniques. Empathy and insight allow salespeople to uncover hidden needs, build trust, and create long-lasting relationships. By combining active listening, relationship-building, and data-driven insights, sales professionals can anticipate client needs and deliver tailored solutions. This chapter will explore these principles and provide actionable steps to integrate them into your sales approach.

Active Listening and Uncovering Hidden Needs

Active listening is the foundation of empathy in sales. It involves fully focusing on the client, understanding their spoken and unspoken needs, and responding thoughtfully.

Key Techniques for Active Listening:

1. Eliminate Distractions:
Focus entirely on the conversation. Avoid checking your phone or thinking about your next response while the client is speaking.

2. Paraphrase and Clarify:
Repeat back key points in your own words to confirm understanding.

3. Read Between the Lines:
Pay attention to tone, body language, and what's left unsaid to uncover deeper concerns.

Example:
During a discovery call, a prospect mentions difficulty scaling their operations but doesn't directly reference budget constraints. By asking follow-up questions like, "What's your biggest concern about scaling right now?" the salesperson uncovers that the client's real issue is maintaining quality while managing costs.

Building Trust and Long-Lasting Relationships

Trust is the cornerstone of successful sales relationships. Building trust requires authenticity, consistency, and a focus on the client's best interests.

Steps to Build Trust:

1. **Be Transparent:** Be honest about what your product can and cannot do.
2. **Follow Through:** Deliver on promises, no matter how small.
3. **Focus on Their Success:** Show genuine interest in helping the client achieve their goals, not just closing a deal.

Example:

A salesperson in the manufacturing industry suggests a lower-priced solution when they realize it better meets the client's needs. While this reduces their immediate commission, it builds trust and leads to a long-term partnership with additional referrals.

Using Data and Analytics to Predict Client Needs

Empathy doesn't just rely on intuition—it can be enhanced with data. By analyzing patterns and behaviors, sales professionals can anticipate client needs and offer proactive solutions.

Leveraging Data Effectively:

1. **CRM Insights:** Use client history and interaction data to identify trends or gaps in their current setup.

2. **Market Trends:** Stay updated on industry shifts that might affect your client's priorities.

3. **Behavioral Analytics:** Monitor client engagement with emails, product usage, or demos to predict readiness to buy.

Example:

A SaaS company notices a client frequently accessing articles on a specific feature in their knowledge base. The salesperson reaches out proactively to discuss upgrading to a plan that includes that feature, addressing the client's interest before they even request it.

Examples of Empathy and Insight in Action

1. Healthcare Technology:

- **Situation:** A hospital administrator complains about long patient wait times but doesn't pinpoint the cause.

- **Empathy:** By actively listening and asking questions, the salesperson learns that scheduling inefficiencies are the root problem.

- **Solution:** They propose an AI-driven scheduling tool, improving wait times by 40%.

2. Retail E-Commerce Platform:

- **Situation:** A client's sales spike during holidays but drop sharply afterward.

- **Data Insight:** Using analytics, the salesperson identifies that abandoned carts are highest during off-peak seasons.

- **Solution:** They recommend implementing targeted follow-up emails, increasing year-round conversions.

Workshop
Activities

1. Active Listening Role-Play
- Pair up participants. One plays the client, sharing a business challenge.
- The salesperson practices active listening by asking clarifying questions and paraphrasing responses.
- Afterward, switch roles and provide feedback on listening skills.

2. Trust-Building Scenarios
- Present participants with hypothetical sales scenarios, such as dealing with a dissatisfied client or recommending a competing solution.
- Discuss how to handle these situations authentically to build trust.

3. Data-Driven Sales Pitch
- Provide a dataset showing a fictional client's behavior (e.g., product usage, website visits).

- Ask participants to craft a proactive sales pitch based on the insights.
- Share pitches with the group and discuss the use of data.

4. Empathy Mapping Exercise

- Create an empathy map for a fictional client, focusing on: What they say, think, feel, and do.
- Use the map to identify hidden needs and brainstorm tailored solutions.

5. Predictive Sales Challenge

- Divide participants into teams and present them with a real-world case study of a company.
- Each team analyzes the company's industry trends and customer behaviors to predict upcoming needs.
- Teams present their predictions and suggested solutions to the group.

Conclusion

Empathy and insight are essential skills for modern sales professionals. By mastering active listening, building trust, and leveraging data analytics, you can connect with clients on a deeper level and anticipate their needs. These skills not only drive sales success but also establish you as a trusted partner who genuinely cares about their clients' goals. Now, it's time to practice these principles and make empathy your competitive edge!

CHAPTER 8

Competitive Analysis and Strategy

> *Knowing your competitors is the first step; differentiating yourself is how you win.*

In today's competitive business landscape, standing out is more challenging than ever. To succeed, sales professionals must think like business owners when analyzing competitors, differentiate their offerings effectively, and build a compelling personal and professional brand. This chapter explores how to gain a competitive edge by understanding the market, leveraging your unique value proposition, and creating a brand that resonates with clients.

How to Analyze Competitors
Like a Business Owner

Business owners view competition strategically, not emotionally. They look beyond surface-level comparisons and analyze the market landscape to identify opportunities.

Steps to Analyze Competitors:

1. **Identify Key Competitors:** Research direct competitors (selling similar products) and indirect competitors (offering alternative solutions to the same problem).

2. **Evaluate Strengths and Weaknesses:** Assess their pricing, product features, market positioning, and customer feedback.

3. **Understand Their Market Strategy:** Study their advertising, partnerships, and client acquisition methods.

4. **Pinpoint Gaps:** Look for unmet client needs or areas where your offering outperforms.

Example:
A salesperson for a cloud storage company identifies that a competitor focuses heavily on enterprise clients but provides limited support for small businesses. By emphasizing their product's affordability and personalized support for small businesses, they tap into an underserved market.

Key Tools for Competitive Analysis:

- **SWOT Analysis:** Identify your competitors' Strengths,

Weaknesses, Opportunities, and Threats.

- **Social Media Monitoring:** Track competitor engagement and campaigns to understand their messaging.
- **Customer Feedback:** Read reviews and testimonials to identify common complaints about competitors.

Differentiating Your Offering in a Crowded Market

Differentiation is about highlighting what makes your product or service unique and why it's the best choice for your clients.

Strategies for Differentiation:

1. **Focus on Value:** Showcase benefits that matter most to your target audience, such as cost savings, time efficiency, or superior quality.
2. **Emphasize Unique Features:** Highlight features competitors can't replicate or those tailored to niche markets.
3. **Deliver Exceptional Service:** Personalize the customer experience, offering something beyond the product itself.

Example:

A sales rep for a marketing automation platform learns that most competitors provide a complex setup process. They emphasize their platform's ease of use and free onboarding support, making it a more attractive option for small marketing teams.

Tailoring Differentiation to the Client:

Adapt your differentiation strategy based on the client's priorities. For example:

- A price-sensitive client values cost-effectiveness.
- A growth-focused client values scalability and ROI.
- A risk-averse client values reliability and support.

Crafting a Personal and
Professional Brand

Your personal brand is your reputation. It's how clients perceive you, your values, and your expertise. Building a strong brand helps establish trust and positions you as a thought leader in your industry.

Steps to Build a Compelling Brand:

1. **Define Your Core Values:** What do you stand for? Transparency, innovation, client success?

2. **Showcase Your Expertise:** Share industry insights, case studies, or educational content on platforms like LinkedIn.

3. **Be Consistent:** Align your online presence, communication style, and actions with your brand values.

4. **Engage Authentically:** Build genuine connections with clients and peers by being approachable and reliable.

Example:
A salesperson in the renewable energy industry builds their brand around sustainability. They post articles about

clean energy trends, attend industry conferences, and highlight how their solutions contribute to environmental goals. Over time, they become a go-to expert for businesses seeking green solutions.

Leveraging Social Proof for Your Brand:

- Collect testimonials from satisfied clients.
- Highlight achievements like awards, certifications, or major deals closed.
- Share client success stories that showcase the impact of your solutions.

Examples of Competitive Strategy in Action

1. Tech Solutions Company:

- **Challenge:** Competing against a larger company with more features.
- **Strategy:** Emphasize their personalized support and faster implementation times.
- **Outcome:** Captures small-to-mid-sized businesses who prioritize speed and service.

2. Luxury Retailer:

- **Challenge:** Competing in a market saturated with premium products.
- **Strategy:** Focus on the exclusivity of their brand and their

unique artisan-crafted designs.

- **Outcome:** Builds loyalty among affluent customers seeking one-of-a-kind items.

3. Freelance Consultant:

- **Challenge:** Competing with established consulting firms.
- **Strategy:** Highlight their agility and ability to offer tailored solutions without the overhead costs of a big firm.
- **Outcome:** Wins clients looking for flexibility and cost-effectiveness.

Workshop
Activities

1. Competitor Analysis Exercise

- Assign participants a fictional or real product and a set of competitors.
- Ask them to perform a SWOT analysis of the competitors.
- Have participants identify one competitive gap their product can fill.

2. Differentiation Pitch Challenge

- Provide participants with a product and a target client profile.
- Have them craft a pitch highlighting what makes the product unique for thatspecific client.
- Present pitches to the group and receive feedback on clarity and impact.

3. Personal Branding Activity

- Ask participants to write a short professional bio emphasizing their unique value as a salesperson.
- Have them share their bios and provide constructive feedback to each other.
- Discuss how they can align their online presence (LinkedIn, email signature, etc.) with their personal brand.

4. Role-Playing: Standing Out in a Competitive Market

- Divide participants into small groups. Each group represents a company pitching the same product to a client.
- The client chooses the most compelling pitch based on differentiation and alignment with their needs.
- Discuss what made the winning pitch stand out.

5. Social Proof Development

- Ask participants to brainstorm ways to collect and leverage testimonials or case studies.
- Develop a short client success story that highlights their product's impact.
- Share and refine these stories in small groups.

Conclusion

Competitive analysis and strategy are essential skills for any salesperson aiming to excel in a crowded market. By thinking like a business owner, tailoring differentiation strategies, and building a personal and professional brand, you can establish yourself as an invaluable partner to your clients. Embrace these tools to stand out, win more deals, and solidify your reputation as a strategic thinker and trusted advisor. Now, take these strategies into your next pitch and see the difference they make!

CHAPTER 9

Taking Ownership in the Sales Process

> *When you treat your territory like your own business, you take control of your success and create opportunities others miss.*

Sales isn't just a job—it's a craft that thrives on ownership, accountability, and continuous growth. Taking ownership means treating your sales territory or market as your own business. It involves proactively making decisions, balancing risks with rewards, and learning from setbacks to improve continuously. This chapter will explore how to adopt an entrepreneurial mindset, embrace calculated risks, and leverage failures as opportunities to refine your approach.

Treating Your Territory or Market as Your Own Business

When you treat your territory or market like a business, you approach it with the strategic mindset of an owner. This means you take full responsibility for outcomes, actively seek opportunities, and operate with the long-term in mind.

Key Actions to Take Ownership:

1. Set Clear Objectives:
Define measurable goals for your territory, such as revenue targets, new client acquisition, or market share growth.

2. Understand Your Market:
Analyze customer segments, industry trends, and competitive landscapes to identify high-priority opportunities.

3. Be Proactive:
Don't wait for leads to come to you. Actively engage with prospects and develop creative strategies to build your pipeline.

4. Track Performance: Regularly monitor key metrics to evaluate progress and adjust your approach.

Example:
Maria, a pharmaceutical sales representative, treated her region like her business. She mapped out her target hospitals and doctors, prioritized those most likely to adopt her products, and scheduled educational seminars to build trust and awareness. Within a year, her territory's revenue grew by 40%, outpacing her peers.

Balancing Risk-Taking with Calculated Decision-Making

Taking ownership often involves stepping outside your comfort zone. However, successful salespeople take calculated risks rather than reckless ones. They evaluate potential outcomes, gather relevant data, and weigh the benefits against the drawbacks.

How to Balance Risk and Reward:

1. Identify Opportunities: Look for trends or gaps in the market where your product can provide unique value.

2. Evaluate the Risk: Ask yourself:
- What's the potential reward?
- What are the consequences of failure?
- Can the risk be mitigated?

3. Start Small: Test new ideas on a smaller scale to reduce risk while gathering valuable feedback.

Example:

Liam, a SaaS salesperson, noticed a new trend among small businesses seeking automation tools. Although his product was traditionally marketed to enterprises, he adapted his pitch to address the needs of small businesses and secured a pilot program with a local startup. The pilot succeeded, and Liam's company expanded into a new customer segment.

Learning from Setbacks and Iterating for Growth

No salesperson closes every deal, and every failure carries lessons. Successful professionals embrace setbacks as opportunities to improve their process.

Steps to Learn and Grow:

1. **Reflect on What Went Wrong:** Analyze the situation honestly. Did you misunderstand the client's needs, face unexpected competition, or fail to follow up effectively?

2. **Seek Feedback:** Ask colleagues, managers, or even clients for constructive input.

3. **Create an Action Plan:** Identify specific steps to improve your approach.

4. **Iterate and Test:** Implement changes, track results, and continue refining your strategy.

Example:

After losing a major deal, Jasmine realized she hadn't fully addressed the client's cost concerns. She worked with her manager to build a clearer ROI framework, which she used in her next presentation. This time, she won the deal and gained the confidence to handle similar objections in the future.

Examples of Ownership
in the Sales Process

1. Industrial Equipment Sales:

- **Challenge:** A salesperson's territory included declining manufacturing companies.
- **Ownership:** They diversified their focus, targeting up-and-coming sectors like renewable energy.
- **Outcome:** They secured partnerships with three solar panel manufacturers, driving significant growth.

2. Real Estate Agent:

- **Challenge:** A slow housing market reduced leads.
- **Ownership:** The agent hosted workshops for first-time buyers, creating a new pipeline of prospects.
- **Outcome:** They closed 15 deals from workshop attendees within six months.

Workshop
Activities

1. Territory Business Plan
- **Exercise:** Have participants create a business plan for their territory or market, including:
  - » Revenue goals.
  - » High-priority prospects or accounts.
  - » Strategies for outreach and growth.

- Share plans in small groups for feedback and refinement.

2. Risk Assessment Simulation

- **Exercise:** Present participants with a hypothetical sales opportunity involving risk (e.g., targeting a new customer segment or pitching a premium solution).
- Ask them to assess the risk and reward, propose a plan, and explain their rationale to the group.

3. Setback Reflection

- **Exercise:** Ask participants to reflect on a recent sales setback and answer these questions:
  - » What went wrong?
  - » What did I learn?
  - » What will I do differently next time?
- Share insights in pairs or small groups to encourage peer learning.

4. Iterative Selling Role-Play

- **Exercise:** Conduct a role-play where participants pitch a product to a difficult client. After receiving feedback, participants revise their approach and try again.
- Discuss how iteration improved their results.

5. Metrics and Tracking Practice

- **Exercise:** Provide a fictional sales scenario with key metrics (e.g., conversion rates, revenue per account).
- Ask participants to analyze the data, identify areas for improvement, and propose an action plan to optimize performance.

Conclusion

Taking ownership of your sales process means adopting an entrepreneurial mindset, proactively making decisions, and continuously improving. By treating your territory or market as your own business, balancing risk with calculated decisions, and learning from setbacks, you can drive consistent growth and establish yourself as a trusted and innovative salesperson. Now, take ownership of your success, and make every action count!

MASTERING THE ART OF INFLUENCE

Section 4 focuses on the advanced skills and strategies that separate great salespeople from good ones. It explores how to craft compelling narratives, leverage psychology to guide decision-making, and negotiate effectively while preserving relationships. This section equips you with tools to communicate persuasively, understand client motivations, and foster trust. By mastering the art of influence, you'll not only close more deals but also create stronger, more meaningful connections with clients.

CHAPTER 10

Persuasive Communication

> "
>
> *Persuasive salespeople use storytelling, psychology, and negotiation to inspire action and foster lasting relationships.*
>
> "

Sales is as much about communication as it is about strategy. Persuasive communication transforms information into action, building connections that inspire trust and drive decisions. In this chapter, we'll explore advanced storytelling techniques, the psychology behind decision-making, and the art of negotiation. By mastering these skills, you can influence outcomes while maintaining strong, long-term relationships with clients.

Advanced Storytelling
Techniques for Sales

Storytelling is one of the most powerful tools in sales. A well-told story engages emotions, simplifies complex concepts, and makes your message memorable. Advanced storytelling techniques go beyond simply sharing anecdotes—they create a vivid, client-centered narrative.

Key Elements of Effective Sales Stories:

1. Relatability: The client must see themselves in the story. Focus on challenges they understand and outcomes they desire.

2. Structure: Follow the classic three-act structure:
- Setup: Introduce the problem or challenge.
- Conflict: Highlight obstacles or risks.
- Resolution: Present your product/service as the hero that solves the problem.

3. Specificity: Include details, such as metrics or client testimonials, to make the story credible and engaging.

Example:

Instead of saying, *"Our product helps save time,"* a salesperson for project management software might tell this story:

"One of our clients, a growing marketing agency, struggled to manage overlapping campaigns. Using our software, they streamlined their processes, saving 20 hours per week. Now, their team spends more time creating content and less time coordinating schedules."

Leveraging Psychology to Influence Decision-Making

Persuasive communication taps into psychological principles that guide how people think and act. Understanding these principles allows you to craft messages that resonate with clients and move them toward action.

Key Psychological Principles for Sales:

1. **Social Proof:** People tend to follow the actions of others. Highlight testimonials, case studies, or statistics to show how others benefit from your solution.

   Example: "85% of businesses in your industry have switched to cloud-based systems—here's why they chose us."

2. **Reciprocity:** When you give something valuable, people feel compelled to give back.

   Example: Offering free consultations or resources builds goodwill and increases the likelihood of a sale.

3. **Scarcity:** Limited availability or exclusivity drives urgency.

   Example: "We're offering this promotion to the first 10 clients who sign up this month."

4. **Anchoring:** Initial information serves as a reference point. Start with a higher-priced option to make subsequent offers seem more reasonable.

   Example: "Our premium package is $10,000, but our standard plan—ideal for your needs—is $7,500."

The Art of Negotiation: Winning Without Compromising Relationships

Negotiation isn't about winning at all costs–it's about creating mutually beneficial agreements that strengthen relationships. The best negotiators find solutions that work for both parties.

Steps to Effective Negotiation:

1. **Prepare Thoroughly:** Understand the client's priorities, potential objections, and decision-making process.

2. **Listen Actively:** Encourage the client to share their concerns and needs. This builds trust and uncovers valuable information.

3. **Focus on Value, Not Price:** Highlight how your solution addresses the client's goals and challenges, shifting the conversation away from cost alone.

4. **Be Willing to Walk Away:** If the terms compromise your product's value or your relationship, it's better to let the deal go.

Example:

A salesperson for a logistics company negotiated a contract with a retailer. When the client demanded a lower price, the salesperson reframed the conversation by emphasizing the value of reduced shipping delays and improved supply chain efficiency. They offered a slight discount in exchange for a longer contract term, resulting in a win-win agreement.

CHAPTER 11

The Psychology of Connecting with All Types of People

"

True connection in sales comes from understanding people—listening to their words, reading their actions, and adapting your approach to build trust, foster empathy, and create lasting relationships.

"

The ability to connect with people is the cornerstone of successful sales. Regardless of personality, communication style, or context, building rapport and trust is essential. But connection goes beyond words—it's about understanding psychology, reading subtle non-verbal cues, and adapting your approach to resonate with different individuals. This chapter explores how to listen actively, interpret body language, identify personality traits, and communicate effectively—all while maintaining composure and fostering positivity.

How to Listen Actively
and Build Trust

Active listening is more than hearing words; it's about fully understanding and validating what the other person is expressing. Clients who feel heard are more likely to trust you and engage in meaningful dialogue.

Steps to Active Listening

1. Eliminate Distractions: Focus entirely on the speaker by silencing your phone, closing unnecessary tabs, and maintaining eye contact.

2. Use Verbal Affirmations: Acknowledge what the person is saying with phrases like, "I see," or "That makes sense."

3. Ask Open-Ended Questions: Encourage elaboration to show genuine interest and uncover deeper insights.

Example: Instead of "Do you like the product?" ask, "How does this product fit into your goals?"

4. Summarize and Reflect: Paraphrase what the person said to confirm understanding.

Example: "So, what I'm hearing is that streamlining this process is your top priority–did I get that right?"

Example in Action
During a meeting, a client expressed concerns about implementation challenges. Instead of jumping in

with solutions, the salesperson listened, summarized their concerns, and asked follow-up questions. This approach allowed the client to feel understood and more open to collaboration.

Reading Non-Verbal Cues

Non-verbal communication often reveals more than words. Learning to read these signals helps you gauge emotions, build rapport, and adapt your approach.

Common Non-Verbal Cues and Their Meanings

1. Eye Contact:

- Steady eye contact suggests confidence and engagement.
- Avoidance can indicate discomfort or disinterest.

2. Body Posture:

- Open posture (uncrossed arms, leaning slightly forward) signals interest.
- Closed posture (crossed arms, leaning back) may indicate resistance.

3. Facial Expressions:

- Smiles often signal agreement or positivity.
- Furrowed brows may indicate confusion or skepticism.

4. Hand Gestures:

- Active gestures often mean enthusiasm.
- Fidgeting or tapping can suggest impatience or nervousness.

How to Use Non-Verbal Cues

- Mirror the client's positive cues to build rapport.
- Address negative cues with empathy.

Example: If a client's arms are crossed, ask, "Do you have any concerns I can clarify?"

Understanding
Personality Traits and
Adapting Your Approach

People have different communication styles, priorities, and decision-making processes. Recognizing personality traits allows you to tailor your message to their preferences.

Four Common Personality Types

1. The Analyst

- **Traits:** Detail-oriented, logical, and cautious.
- **How to Sell:** Provide data, case studies, and a clear, step-by-step explanation.

2. The Operative

- **Traits:** Goal-oriented, decisive, and focused on results.
- **How to Sell:** Be direct, focus on outcomes, and avoid unnecessary small talk.

3. The Diplomat

- **Traits:** Relationship-focused, empathetic, and hesitant to take risks.
- **How to Sell:** Build trust through personal connection and emphasize how your solution aligns with their values.

4. The General

- **Traits:** Energetic, creative, and big-picture thinkers.
- **How to Sell:** Use storytelling, share bold ideas, and highlight how your solution drives innovation.

How to Talk So
They Will Listen

Effective communication is about making your message resonate. This requires clarity, empathy, and alignment with the client's priorities.

Steps to Speak Effectively

1. Use Their Language: Reflect the client's terminology to show alignment.

> **Example:** If they refer to "cost optimization" instead of "savings," mirror their wording.

2. Focus on Value: Emphasize how your solution addresses their specific needs and goals.

3. Keep It Concise: Avoid overwhelming your audience with excessive details—focus on what matters most.

How to Maintain Composure and Foster Positivity

Sales is often unpredictable, and staying calm under pressure is a key skill. Maintaining composure not only protects your credibility but also allows you to think clearly and respond effectively.

Why Staying Calm Matters

1. Regulates Emotions:
Clients pick up on your energy—calmness fosters trust.

2. Improves Problem-Solving: A clear mind helps you navigate challenges more effectively.

How to Stay Calm When Feeling Upset

1. Recognize the Trigger:
When you feel frustration rising, pause and identify the source.

2. Take a Deep Breath:
A few deep breaths lower stress and reset your mindset.

3. Reframe the Situation:
Shift your focus to problem-solving rather than dwelling on the problem itself.

Example:
Instead of thinking, "Why is this client being difficult?" ask, "What can I do to make them feel more at ease?"

How to Be Nice Without Being Passive

Niceness in sales is about showing respect and empathy without compromising assertiveness.

1. Be Polite: Use positive language and express gratitude.

2. Set Boundaries Respectfully: Assert your position without aggression.

> **Example:** "I'd love to help, but here's what I need to make this work for both of us."

Workshop
Activities

1. Non-Verbal Cue Practice

- **Activity:** Pair participants and have one express emotions (e.g., enthusiasm, doubt) using only non-verbal cues. The other identifies the emotion and responds appropriately.
- **Objective:** Improve recognition and response to non-verbal signals.

2. Personality Type Role-Play

- **Activity:** Assign participants different personality traits (e.g., Analyst, Operative) and have others adapt their pitch to suit that type.
- **Objective:** Practice tailoring communication styles.

3. Staying Calm Simulation

- **Activity:** Present participants with a challenging scenario (e.g., an angry client or unexpected objection) and have them practice staying composed and redirecting the conversation.
- **Objective:** Build resilience and composure under pressure.

Conclusion

Connecting with people in sales isn't just about knowing your product—it's about understanding human behavior. By listening actively, reading non-verbal cues, adapting to personality traits, and staying calm, you can build stronger relationships and close more deals. Practice these skills daily, and you'll become a master of connection and communication.

CHAPTER 12

Leadership in Sales

> **"**
>
> *True sales leadership means guiding clients to solutions, empowering peers, and driving success for everyone around you.*
>
> **"**

Sales is more than hitting quotas and closing deals; it's about leading clients to the right solutions, inspiring your peers, and driving collective success. Leadership in sales doesn't require a managerial title—it's a mindset and a set of skills that elevate your performance and the performance of those around you. This chapter explores how sales professionals can adopt leadership thinking to guide clients, mentor colleagues, and enhance their impact in the organization.

Leading Clients to Solutions, Not Just Closing Deals

The best salespeople don't focus solely on closing deals; they prioritize delivering value by guiding clients to the right solutions. This client-first mindset builds trust, fosters long-term relationships, and often results in repeat business and referrals.

Key Practices for Leading Clients:

1. Understand the Client's Goals:
Look beyond the immediate transaction to understand the client's long-term objectives.

2. Ask Thoughtful Questions:
Use open-ended questions to uncover deeper needs and challenges.

3. Provide Insight:
Position yourself as an expert by offering solutions that align with their strategy, even if it means recommending an alternative product or service.

Example:
A B2B software salesperson realizes during a pitch that the client's current infrastructure won't support their top-tier product. Instead of pushing the sale, they recommend a more affordable solution to meet the client's current needs, while outlining a growth path for future upgrades. The client appreciates the honesty and becomes a loyal customer.

Mentoring and Empowering Your Peers for Collective Success

True leaders lift others. In a sales team, mentoring and empowering peers enhances collaboration, improves morale, and drives better results for the entire organization.

Ways to Mentor and Empower:

1. Share Knowledge:
Offer tips, strategies, and insights gained from your own experience.

2. Encourage Collaboration:
Promote a team-oriented culture where successes are shared, not siloed.

3. Celebrate Wins:
Acknowledge your peers' achievements to build confidence and camaraderie.

4. Provide Constructive Feedback:
Help colleagues identify growth opportunities with kindness and actionable advice.

Example:
After becoming a top performer, Samantha regularly shares her strategies in team meetings, including how she approaches objections and builds rapport. Her openness inspires the team to improve, and the entire group surpasses its quarterly targets.

How Leadership Thinking
Enhances Sales Performance

Leadership thinking encourages salespeople to adopt a broader perspective, seeing their role as part of a larger mission to deliver value to clients and contribute to the team's success. This mindset leads to more strategic decisions, better relationships, and a stronger sense of purpose.

Benefits of Leadership Thinking:

1. Enhanced Problem-Solving:
Leaders focus on finding solutions rather than dwelling on obstacles.

2. Increased Credibility:
Clients trust sales professionals who demonstrate confidence, expertise, and integrity.

3. Better Team Dynamics:
A leadership mindset fosters collaboration and reduces unhealthy competition.

4. Long-Term Success:
Leadership-oriented salespeople build stronger client relationships and are more likely to be promoted within their organizations.

Example:
Mark consistently takes initiative to improve his sales team's processes, from suggesting new CRM workflows to organizing peer-led training sessions. His leadership boosts team efficiency and earns him recognition, leading to his promotion as team lead.

Examples of
Leadership in Sales

1. Enterprise Sales Executive:

» **Challenge:** A client struggled to articulate their needs for a large-scale software purchase.

» **Leadership:** The salesperson guided them through a needs assessment, helping the client prioritize features and make an informed decision.

» **Outcome:** The client chose the solution with confidence, leading to a multi-year contract.

2. Small Business Consultant:

» **Challenge:** A team member struggled with cold calling, lowering their confidence.

» **Leadership:** The consultant offered one-on-one coaching, sharing techniques that had worked for them.

» **Outcome:** The team member's performance improved, and they secured their first major account.

Workshop
Activities

1. Client Leadership Role-Play

• **Exercise:** Pair participants for a role-play where one acts as the client and the other as the salesperson.

- The client presents a vague or complex challenge, and the salesperson must lead them to a clear, actionable solution.
- Rotate roles and provide feedback on communication and problem-solving skills.

2. Mentoring Simulation

- **Exercise:** Assign participants to mentor a peer who is struggling with a specific sales skill (e.g., handling objections, closing deals).
- The mentor provides advice, shares a relevant story, and role-plays the scenario with their mentee.
- Debrief to discuss the effectiveness of the mentoring approach.

3. Leadership Reflection Exercise

- **Exercise:** Ask participants to reflect on a time when they demonstrated leadership in their sales role.
- Have them write down:
  » The challenge they faced.
  » The actions they took.
  » The outcome and lessons learned.
- Share stories in small groups to inspire others.

4. Team Collaboration Challenge

- **Exercise:** Divide participants into teams and give them a complex sales challenge (e.g., developing a strategy for a high-profile client).
- Teams must work together to propose a solution, with each member contributing their expertise.
- Present solutions and discuss how teamwork and leadership shaped the outcomes.

5. Creating a Leadership Action Plan

- **Exercise:** Ask participants to outline specific steps they can take to demonstrate leadership in their sales role, including:
  - » How they will lead clients to solutions.
  - » How they will mentor or empower peers.
  - » How they will adopt leadership thinking in their daily work.
- Share and refine these action plans in small groups.

Conclusion

Leadership in sales is about guiding clients, inspiring peers, and driving positive change within your organization. By adopting a leadership mindset, you elevate not only your own performance but also the success of your clients and team. Leadership isn't about titles—it's about taking initiative, acting with integrity, and delivering value in every interaction. With the skills and practices in this chapter, you can become a sales leader who creates lasting impact and inspires others to achieve their best. Now, step into your leadership role and make a difference!

SUSTAINING PEAK PERFORMANCE

Sustaining success in sales requires more than short-term wins—it demands balance, continuous improvement, and a commitment to building a legacy. Section 5 emphasizes the importance of work-life balance to avoid burnout, continuous learning to stay competitive, and replicable strategies to ensure consistent results. These chapters provide a roadmap for achieving long-term success while maintaining your health, happiness, and passion for the craft. By embracing sustainable practices and sharing your knowledge, you'll leave a lasting impact on your career and the sales profession.

CHAPTER 13

Continuous Learning and Self-Improvement

―― " ――

To stay ahead, you must never stop learning, adapting, and evolving with the ever-changing world of sales.

―― " ――

The most successful sales professionals embrace learning as a lifelong journey. Continuous self-improvement is essential for staying competitive, adapting to industry changes, and delivering exceptional value to clients. In this chapter, we'll explore how to stay ahead of trends, leverage technology and AI, and use feedback and self-assessment as tools for growth. By developing a mindset of curiosity and adaptability, you can remain at the forefront of your field and consistently outperform your competition.

Staying Ahead of Industry Trends and Innovations

The business landscape evolves rapidly, and sales professionals who stay informed about industry trends gain a significant competitive edge. Understanding innovations and emerging challenges positions you as a thought leader and allows you to anticipate client needs.

Strategies for Staying Informed:

1. Read and Research Regularly:
Follow industry publications, blogs, and newsletters to stay updated on trends.

2. Attend Events and Webinars:
Industry conferences, webinars, and networking events provide insights and connections.

3. Engage with Thought Leaders:
Follow experts on social media, read their books, and listen to their podcasts.

4. Monitor Competitors:
Study how competitors are adapting to trends and use that information to refine your strategy.

Example:
A salesperson in the renewable energy sector noticed the growing demand for energy storage solutions by following industry reports. They proactively educated themselves about battery technology, enabling them to pitch new solutions to clients before competitors did.

Leveraging Technology and AI to Augment Sales Strategies

Technology and artificial intelligence (AI) are transforming the sales process, offering tools that enhance efficiency, accuracy, and personalization. Sales professionals who adopt these tools can focus more on relationship-building and strategy.

Ways to Leverage Technology and AI:

1. CRM Tools:
Use customer relationship management software to track interactions, manage leads, and analyze data.

2. Sales Automation:
Automate repetitive tasks like follow-up emails, lead scoring, and scheduling to save time.

3. AI-Driven Insights:
Use AI tools to predict customer behavior, identify cross-selling opportunities, and personalize outreach.

4. Learning Platforms:
Access online courses and certifications to develop new skills and stay ahead of technological advancements.

Example:
A B2B salesperson used an AI-powered sales tool to analyze client data and identify accounts most likely to renew contracts. By focusing on these accounts, they increased their retention rate by 25% while reducing the time spent on unqualified leads.

The Importance of Feedback and Self-Assessment

Feedback and self-assessment are critical for identifying blind spots, celebrating strengths, and driving continuous improvement. Top-performing salespeople actively seek input and reflect on their performance.

How to Use Feedback Effectively:

1. Ask for Specific Feedback:
Request actionable insights from managers, peers, and clients.

2. Be Open and Receptive:
Approach feedback with curiosity, not defensiveness.

3. Implement Changes:
Turn feedback into specific actions for improvement.

Self-Assessment Techniques:

1. Review Performance Metrics:
Regularly analyze your KPIs to identify areas of success and improvement.

2. Record and Review Calls:
Listening to your own sales calls helps identify strengths and areas to refine.

3. Set Personal Benchmarks:
Compare your performance against past results to measure growth.

> **Example:**
> After receiving feedback from a client about overly technical explanations, a software sales rep adjusted their pitch to focus on user-friendly benefits. This shift improved their close rate by 15% and enhanced client satisfaction.

Examples of Continuous Learning and Self-Improvement

1. SaaS Sales Professional:

- **Challenge:** Keeping up with rapidly changing product updates.

- **Solution:** Dedicated 30 minutes daily to product training and used internal knowledge bases to stay informed.

- **Outcome:** Closed larger deals by demonstrating deeper product expertise.

2. Healthcare Sales Rep:

- **Challenge:** Addressing client concerns about new regulations.

- **Solution**: Attended industry webinars and collaborated with legal teams to stay compliant and informed.

- **Outcome:** Became a trusted advisor to clients navigating regulatory changes.

Workshop

Activities

1. Trend Tracking Exercise

- **Exercise:** Provide participants with access to industry reports or articles.
- Ask them to identify one emerging trend and brainstorm how it could affect their clients or territory.
- Share insights with the group to create a collective knowledge base.

2. AI Tools Exploration

- **Exercise:** Assign participants to research and demo an AI sales tool relevant to their role (e.g., predictive analytics, automated outreach).
- Ask them to present how the tool could improve their sales strategy and efficiency.

3. Feedback Role-Play

- **Exercise:** In pairs, participants take turns acting as the salesperson and the feedback provider.
- The salesperson presents a recent challenge, and the feedback provider offers constructive insights.
- Discuss how feedback was delivered and received.

4. Self-Assessment Action Plan

- **Exercise:** Have participants complete a self-assessment, rating themselves on skills like product knowledge, communication, and closing techniques.

- Based on their results, ask them to set three specific improvement goals and outline action steps.
- Share plans in small groups for accountability.

5. Technology Brainstorm

- **Exercise:** Divide participants into small groups and ask them to brainstorm how technology (e.g., CRM tools, analytics platforms) can solve a specific sales challenge, such as lead prioritization or client follow-up.
- Each group presents their solution to the workshop.

Conclusion

Continuous learning and self-improvement are not optional for successful sales professionals—they are essential. Staying ahead of industry trends, leveraging technology, and seeking feedback are the keys to adapting and thriving in an ever-changing landscape. By embracing a growth mindset and making learning a priority, you'll remain competitive, enhance your skills, and deliver more value to your clients. Now, take the tools and techniques from this chapter and commit to becoming a lifelong learner in your sales journey.

CHAPTER 14

Work-Life Balance for Long-Term Success

"

Success means nothing without balance—invest in your well-being to thrive both personally and professionally.

"

Sales can be exhilarating, but it's also one of the most demanding professions. The pressure to meet targets, maintain client relationships, and stay competitive can lead to burnout if not managed effectively. Achieving work-life balance is essential for sustaining long-term success. This chapter explores strategies to avoid burnout, build sustainable routines, and cultivate fulfilling relationships and hobbies outside of work. By prioritizing balance, you'll protect your health, maintain productivity, and enjoy a richer, more fulfilling life.

Avoiding Burnout in High-Pressure Sales Environments

Burnout is a state of emotional, physical, and mental exhaustion caused by prolonged stress. In sales, burnout often arises from overworking, unrealistic expectations, or neglecting self-care. Recognizing the signs and taking proactive steps can prevent burnout from derailing your career.

Signs of Burnout:

1. Chronic Fatigue:
Feeling drained even after rest.

2. Decreased Performance:
Struggling to meet goals or stay focused.

3. Emotional Detachment:
Losing interest in your work or clients.

How to Prevent Burnout:

1. Set Boundaries:
Define clear start and end times for your workday and stick to them.

2. Learn to Say No:
Prioritize tasks that align with your goals and delegate or decline others.

3. Take Breaks:
Regularly step away from work to recharge.

Example:

Laura, a high-performing account executive, began feeling overwhelmed by constant client demands. She implemented "focus hours" in her schedule, during which she turned off notifications and concentrated on high-priority tasks. She also started taking 30-minute walks during lunch. These changes improved her productivity and reduced her stress levels.

Building a Sustainable Routine for Health and Productivity

A sustainable routine supports both your professional performance and personal well-being. It's about creating habits that optimize energy, focus, and resilience.

Key Components of a Sustainable Routine:

1. Prioritize Sleep:
Aim for 7-8 hours of quality sleep to improve focus and decision-making.

2. Exercise Regularly:
Incorporate physical activity to boost energy and reduce stress.

3. Plan Your Day:
Use tools like calendars or task managers to organize your

time effectively.

4. Practice Mindfulness:
Dedicate time to activities like meditation or journaling to stay grounded.

Example:

David, a sales manager, struggled with scattered priorities and late-night emails. He adopted a morning routine that included 10 minutes of meditation, a 20-minute workout, and reviewing his top three tasks for the day. This routine improved his focus and allowed him to disconnect after work.

Cultivating Relationships and Hobbies Outside of Work

A fulfilling life outside of work is key to maintaining balance and avoiding burnout. Relationships and hobbies provide emotional support, creative outlets, and a sense of identity beyond your career.

Nurturing Relationships:

1. Make Time for Loved Ones:
Schedule regular time with family and friends, even if it's brief.

2. Be Present:
When spending time with others, put away work distractions and focus on meaningful interactions.

3. Build a Support Network:
Connect with peers who understand your challenges and can offer advice or encouragement.

Engaging in Hobbies:

1. Choose Activities You Love:
Find hobbies that energize or relax you, whether it's cooking, painting, or hiking.

2. Schedule Time for Fun:
Treat hobbies as non-negotiable appointments in your calendar.

3. Learn Something New:
Exploring new interests keeps you curious and resilient.

Example:
Michelle, a real estate agent, found herself consumed by work. She joined a local running club, which gave her a structured outlet for stress relief and introduced her to new friends. This balanced her schedule and improved her overall happiness.

Examples of Work-Life Balance in Action

1. Tech Sales Rep:

- **Challenge:** Constantly checking emails after hours.
- **Solution:** Set a strict "no work after 9 PM" rule
- **Outcome:** Improved mental health and better focus during work hours.

2. Healthcare Consultant:

- **Challenge:** Neglecting personal health during busy seasons.
- **Solution:** Committed to morning yoga sessions and meal prepping on Sundays.
- **Outcome:** Increased energy and reduced stress during high-pressure periods.

3. Retail Sales Manager:

- **Challenge:** Losing touch with friends due to long hours.
- **Solution:** Scheduled monthly meetups with friends to reconnect.
- **Outcome:** Strengthened relationships and gained emotional support.

Workshop
Activities

1. Identifying Burnout Triggers

- **Exercise:** Ask participants to reflect on the past month and list three situations that caused significant stress or fatigue.
- Discuss strategies to address or prevent these triggers moving forward.

2. Designing a Sustainable Routine

- **Exercise:** Have participants outline their ideal daily routine, including time for work, exercise, hobbies, and rest.

- Share routines in small groups and provide feedback on how to make them more
- sustainable.

3. Work-Life Balance Wheel

- **Exercise:** Create a wheel with segments representing areas of life (e.g., work, health, family, hobbies).
- Ask participants to rate their satisfaction in each area from 1 to 10 and identify areas needing improvement.
- Discuss strategies to create balance across all areas.

4. Building a Support Network

- **Exercise:** Ask participants to list people in their personal and professional lives who support them.
- Brainstorm ways to strengthen these relationships and expand their network.

5. Hobby Brainstorm

- **Exercise:** Divide participants into groups and ask them to brainstorm hobbies or activities they've always wanted to try.
- Have them share why these activities appeal to them and set a goal to pursue one new hobby within the next month.

Conclusion

Work-life balance is essential for sustaining success in sales. By avoiding burnout, building a sustainable routine, and cultivating meaningful relationships and hobbies, you can maintain your health, productivity, and happiness over the long term. Sales is a marathon, not a sprint, and prioritizing balance will ensure you perform at your best while enjoying a fulfilling life outside of work. Now, take a step back, reflect on your priorities, and commit to making balance a key part of your sales journey.

CHAPTER 15

Measuring and Replicating Success

"

Success isn't luck; it's a system you measure, refine, and share to achieve consistent results and leave a legacy.

"

Success in sales isn't just about achieving results—it's about understanding how you got there and creating a framework to replicate and scale those outcomes. By setting measurable goals and key performance indicators (KPIs), developing repeatable processes, and sharing your knowledge, you can achieve consistent results and leave a lasting legacy in sales. This chapter explores how to measure success effectively, build systems for long-term performance, and contribute to the success of others.

Setting Measurable Goals and Key Performance Indicators (KPIs)

Measurable goals and KPIs provide clarity and focus. They help you understand what's working, what's not, and where to direct your efforts. Effective goals are specific, measurable, achievable, relevant, and time-bound (SMART).

How to Set Measurable Goals:

1. Define Clear Objectives:
Focus on what you want to achieve (e.g., increase revenue, acquire new clients, improve client retention).

2. Break Down Big Goals:
Divide larger objectives into smaller, actionable steps.

3. Track Progress Regularly:
Use dashboards or reports to monitor your performance.

Common KPIs in Sales:

- **Revenue Growth:** Total revenue generated in a given period.

- **Conversion Rate:** Percentage of leads converted to customers.

- **Client Retention:** Percentage of clients who renew or continue their contracts.

- **Sales Cycle Length:** Average time taken to close a deal.

- **Lead Response Time:** Time it takes to follow up with a lead.

Example:

Emma, a real estate agent, set a goal to close 20% more deals this quarter. She broke it down into weekly KPIs, including 10 new client meetings and 20 follow-up calls per week. Tracking these metrics allowed her to stay on course and exceed her goal by 25%.

Building Repeatable Processes for Consistent Results

Repeatable processes ensure that success isn't accidental—it's intentional and scalable. A well-defined process reduces guesswork and increases efficiency.

Steps to Build Repeatable Processes:

1. Document What Works:

Identify the strategies and techniques that lead to success and document them step by step.

2. Standardize Your Workflow:

Create templates, scripts, or checklists for tasks like client onboarding, pitching, and follow-ups.

3. Automate Where Possible:

Use technology to streamline repetitive tasks, such as email outreach or data entry.

4. Test and Refine:

Regularly review your processes to identify areas for improvement.

> **Example:**
> A SaaS sales team noticed their top reps consistently followed up with leads within 24 hours. They turned this into a standard process for the entire team, which led to a 15% increase in conversion rates.

Sharing Your Knowledge
to Leave a Legacy in Sales

Great salespeople don't just focus on their own success—they inspire and empower others. Sharing your knowledge and experiences can elevate your team, build your professional reputation, and create a lasting impact.

Ways to Share Your Knowledge:

1. Mentor Colleagues:
Guide new or struggling team members by sharing best practices and offering support.

2. Host Training Sessions:
Lead workshops or lunch-and-learns to teach specific skills.

3. Create Resources:
Develop guides, templates, or playbooks based on your expertise.

4. Celebrate Team Success:
Acknowledge and share stories of collective wins to foster collaboration.

Example:

After becoming a top performer, Liam created a guide on overcoming objections and shared it with his team. His insights helped several colleagues improve their close rates, and the team collectively achieved record-breaking results.

Examples of Measuring and Replicating Success

1. E-Commerce Sales Manager:

- **Challenge:** Inconsistent follow-up processes led to missed opportunities.
- **Solution:** Developed a standardized follow-up template and integrated it into the CRM.
- **Outcome:** Reduced lead response time by 30% and increased conversions by 20%.

2. Financial Services Consultant:

- **Challenge:** Difficulty tracking which activities led to new client acquisition.
- **Solution:** Implemented a KPI dashboard to measure weekly outreach, meetings, and proposals.
- **Outcome:** Identified that personalized proposals had the highest success rate and scaled this strategy across the team.

3. Retail Sales Associate:

- **Challenge:** New hires struggled with upselling premium products.
- **Solution:** Created a training module focused on value-based selling techniques.
- **Outcome:** New hires improved their average transaction value by 15% within three months.

Workshop
Activities

1. SMART Goal Setting (Specific, Measurable, Achievable, Relevant & Time Bound)

- **Exercise:** Ask participants to set one SMART goal for the next quarter.
- Break it into weekly and daily tasks.
- Share goals with the group for feedback and accountability.

2. KPI Dashboard Design

- **Exercise:** Provide participants with a fictional sales scenario.
- Have them identify the most important KPIs and create a simple dashboard to track progress.
- Discuss how these metrics drive decision-making.

3. Process Mapping

- **Exercise:** Have participants map out a successful sales process they've used, step by step.

- Pair participants to review each other's processes and identify opportunities for improvement or scalability.

4. Knowledge Sharing Session

- **Exercise:** Ask participants to prepare a short presentation on a sales technique or strategy that has worked for them.
- Presentations should include specific examples and results.
- Compile the presentations into a shared resource for the group.

5. Success Replication Brainstorm

- **Exercise:** Divide participants into groups and provide a case study of a successful sales campaign.
- Ask them to identify which elements can be replicated and how they would apply the lessons to a different scenario.
- Present findings to the group.

Conclusion

Measuring and replicating success ensures that your achievements are not only sustainable but scalable. By setting measurable goals, building repeatable processes, and sharing your knowledge, you can continuously improve your performance while uplifting those around you. Success isn't a one-time event—it's a system you build and refine over time. Commit to mastering these principles, and you'll leave a legacy of excellence and impact in the world of sales. Now, go measure your success, refine your strategies, and help others rise along with you!

CHAPTER 16

Confidence, Action, and Managing Up

> *Confidence fuels your potential, action turns plans into results, and managing up ensures you're always aligned with leadership to drive meaningful impact.*

Confidence, decisive action, and the ability to manage upward relationships are critical skills for any sales professional aiming to excel. Confidence fuels your ability to connect with clients and present solutions persuasively. Taking action transforms plans into results. Managing up ensures alignment with leadership, access to resources, and the ability to influence key decisions. In this chapter, we'll explore how to build unshakable confidence, develop an action-oriented mindset, and manage upward relationships to maximize your potential in sales and beyond.

Maximizing Confidence

Confidence isn't just a personality trait—it's a skill that can be developed and strengthened through deliberate practice. In sales, confidence inspires trust, reassures clients, and empowers you to handle objections effectively.

Building Confidence in Sales

1. Master Your Product and Market Knowledge
Confidence comes from knowing your material. The better you understand your product, market, and competitors, the more assured you'll feel in any interaction.

Tip: Schedule regular updates with your team or industry resources to stay informed.

2. Practice Your Pitch
Repetition builds mastery. Role-play scenarios, rehearse responses to objections, and refine your delivery to sound polished and natural.

Tip: Record yourself pitching and review your tone, pace, and content to identify areas for improvement.

3. Celebrate Small Wins
Confidence grows with success. Acknowledge even small victories, like scheduling a follow-up meeting or receiving positive feedback, to keep your momentum.

4. Reframe Rejection
Rejection is a natural part of sales, not a personal failure. Use it as an opportunity to learn and refine your approach.

Tip: After a rejection, ask yourself: "What can I do differently next time?"

> ### Example
>
> A sales rep new to SaaS was intimidated by technical conversations with clients. They invested time in product training, practiced pitches with colleagues, and celebrated small wins like answering a difficult question effectively. Over time, their confidence grew, and they became a top performer.

Taking Decisive Action

Sales professionals who succeed are those who act decisively. Overthinking can lead to missed opportunities, while taking action, even imperfectly, creates momentum and results.

How to Develop an Action-Oriented Mindset

1. Prioritize and Execute

Focus on high-impact activities that move the needle. Create a daily action plan and tackle the most critical tasks first.

Tip: Use the 80/20 rule—80% of your results often come from 20% of your efforts.

2. Adopt a "Fail Forward" Mentality

Understand that mistakes are part of growth. Take calculated risks and treat every action as a learning opportunity.

Tip: Set weekly goals that stretch your comfort zone, such as pitching a new product or targeting a new client segment.

3. Stop Waiting for Perfect Conditions

There's never a "perfect time" to act. Take the first step, refine your approach, and adjust as needed.

Tip: If you're unsure how to proceed, ask, "What's the smallest step I can take right now?"

Example

A real estate agent hesitated to call high-net-worth prospects due to imposter syndrome. Instead of waiting to feel fully prepared, they created a simple script and made one call a day. Within a month, they booked three high-value meetings and closed a major sale.

Managing Up for
Alignment and Influence

Managing up is about building productive relationships with leadership, ensuring alignment with company goals, and securing support for your initiatives. When done effectively, managing up allows you to influence decisions and create opportunities for growth.

Strategies for Managing Up

1. Understand Leadership Priorities

Learn what matters most to your manager or leadership team—whether it's hitting revenue targets, expanding market share, or improving client retention.

Tip: Ask open-ended questions like, "What's your top priority this quarter, and how can I contribute?"

2. Communicate Proactively

Keep leadership informed about your progress, challenges, and ideas. Regular updates build trust and ensure alignment.

Tip: Use concise, results-focused summaries in emails or meetings to highlight key points.

3. Anticipate Needs

Think one step ahead. Anticipate potential challenges or opportunities and propose solutions before they become pressing issues.

Tip: If you notice a trend affecting your team's performance, offer actionable recommendations for addressing it.

4. Bring Solutions, Not Just Problems

Leaders value problem-solvers. When presenting a challenge, always suggest at least one possible solution.

Tip: If a client's demand is affecting your quota, propose a strategy for reallocating resources or adjusting timelines.

Example

A sales manager noticed their team was struggling with a new CRM tool. Instead of waiting for leadership to intervene, they documented key pain points and proposed a training program. Leadership approved, and the team's productivity improved by 20%.

1. Confidence Builder Role-Play

- **Activity:** In pairs, role-play challenging sales scenarios, such as handling tough objections or negotiating pricing. Rotate roles and provide feedback on delivery and tone.
- **Objective:** Build confidence through practice and constructive critique.

2. Action Plan Creation

- **Activity:** Ask participants to identify one area where they've been hesitant to act. Create a 3-step action plan to address it, with specific deadlines.
- **Objective:** Encourage decisive action and accountability.

3. Managing Up Simulation

- **Activity:** In groups, participants simulate a scenario where they need to present a challenge to leadership. Each participant must propose a solution and explain its benefits.
- **Objective:** Practice framing ideas effectively for leadership buy-in.

4. Rejection Reframe Exercise

- **Activity:** Write down a recent rejection or failure. In groups, discuss what lessons were learned and how they can be applied to future opportunities.

- **Objective:** Shift perspective on setbacks to see them as growth opportunities.

Conclusion

Maximizing confidence, taking action, and mastering upward management are three pillars of sustained success in sales. By building confidence, you project trust and credibility. By taking action, you create momentum and results. And by managing up, you align with leadership and position yourself as a valued contributor. These skills aren't just about sales— they're about becoming a leader in any environment.

The Future of Sales Performance

--- ❝ ---

The future of sales belongs to those who embrace innovation, build meaningful connections, and think like owners to stay ahead in a changing world.

--- ❞ ---

As the world continues to evolve, so does the sales profession. Emerging technologies, shifting buyer behaviors, and economic challenges are reshaping the landscape. Yet, amidst all these changes, the core principles of sales—human connection, value creation, and ownership thinking—remain critical. This chapter explores the trends shaping the future of sales, why human connection will always be a cornerstone, and how thinking like a business owner will keep salespeople competitive in any market.

Trends Shaping the Future of Sales

1. AI and Automation

- **What's Happening:** Artificial intelligence and automation tools are transforming prospecting, lead scoring, and client outreach.
- **Impact:** Repetitive tasks are being streamlined, allowing salespeople to focus on high-value activities like relationship-building and strategy.
- **Example:** A SaaS sales team uses AI-driven tools to analyze client data, identifying warm leads faster and enabling personalized outreach at scale.

2. Virtual and Hybrid Selling

- **What's Happening:** The shift to remote work has made virtual selling a standard practice. Buyers now expect digital interactions to be seamless and effective.
- **Impact:** Salespeople need to master virtual communication tools and techniques to create meaningful connections online.
- **Example:** A pharmaceutical rep uses virtual reality demos to showcase equipment, providing an immersive experience without in-person meetings.

3. Data-Driven Decision Making

- **What's Happening:** Advanced analytics are enabling sales teams to predict client behavior, identify market trends, and measure performance with precision.
- **Impact:** Data is becoming a key competitive advantage,

but sales professionals must learn to interpret and apply insights effectively.

- **Example:** A B2B rep analyzes purchase patterns to recommend the right upsell products, increasing average order value by 15%.

4. Focus on Sustainability

- **What's Happening:** Businesses and consumers are increasingly prioritizing sustainable and socially responsible practices.
- **Impact:** Salespeople who align their pitches with clients' sustainability goals will stand out.
- **Example:** A logistics company highlights its eco-friendly shipping options, helping clients meet their carbon reduction targets.

Why Human Connection Will Remain at the Heart of Sales

While technology enhances efficiency, it can't replace the trust and rapport built through human interaction. Buyers still value empathy, understanding, and a personal touch—qualities that machines cannot replicate.

The Role of Empathy

- **Why It Matters:** Buyers want to feel understood, not just sold to. Salespeople who actively listen and address emotional and practical needs will foster stronger relationships.
- **Example:** A salesperson closes a deal not by pushing a

product but by empathizing with the client's concerns and offering a tailored solution.

The Importance of Trust

- **Why It Matters:** Automation can deliver information, but trust is built through consistent, transparent, and ethical behavior.
- **Example:** A client chooses a vendor they've worked with for years over a cheaper alternative because of their proven reliability.

Blending Technology with Humanity

- **Why It Matters:** Tools like AI can provide insights, but it's the salesperson's ability to interpret and act on those insights that drives results.
- **Example:** A sales rep uses AI to identify a client's preferences but adds value by discussing those insights during a personal call, deepening the relationship.

The Enduring Value of Thinking Like an Owner in Any Market

The future of sales will continue to reward those who approach their work with an entrepreneurial mindset. Thinking like an owner means being proactive, strategic, and client-focused.

Key Benefits of Ownership Thinking:

1. Adaptability:
Owners pivot quickly when market conditions change. Salespeople with this mindset can innovate in response to new challenges.

Example: A retail salesperson shifts their focus to e-commerce solutions during a market downturn, capitalizing on online sales growth.

2. Value Creation:
Owners focus on delivering value beyond the immediate transaction. Sales professionals who align their solutions with long-term client goals will stand out.

Example: A consultant helps a client implement a strategy that saves them money now and positions them for growth in the future.

3. Sustainability:
Owners build for the long term. By nurturing relationships and improving processes, salespeople can create lasting success.

Example: A territory manager invests in consistent follow-ups and client education, leading to higher retention rates and referrals.

Workshop
Activities

1. Trend Impact Brainstorm

- **Exercise:** Divide participants into groups and assign each a trend (e.g., AI, virtual selling, sustainability).
- Have them discuss how this trend will affect their sales strategies and present actionable ideas for adapting to it.

2. Human Connection Role-Play

- **Exercise:** In pairs, participants role-play a sales scenario where one person uses technology-driven insights but adds a personal touch to the conversation.
- Rotate roles and provide feedback on how well empathy and trust were demonstrated.

3. Owner's Mindset Challenge

- **Exercise:** Present participants with a fictional sales territory and a list of challenges (e.g., declining market, new competition).
- Ask them to develop an "owner's strategy" for overcoming these challenges and achieving growth.
- Share strategies with the group.

4. Building Hybrid Selling Skills

- **Exercise:** Have participants practice delivering a pitch virtually, using tools like screen sharing and video conferencing.

- Provide feedback on how effectively they engaged the client and conveyed their message.

5. Personalized Sales Plan

- **Exercise:** Ask participants to create a personalized sales strategy that incorporates trends like data-driven insights or sustainability.
- Share plans in small groups and refine based on feedback.

Conclusion

The future of sales will be shaped by emerging technologies and evolving client expectations, but its foundation will remain rooted in human connection and strategic thinking. Sales professionals who embrace these trends, leverage tools wisely, and think like business owners will thrive in any market. The combination of empathy, innovation, and an entrepreneurial mindset will set you apart as a leader in your field. Now, it's time to take these principles, adapt them to your journey, and lead the future of sales with confidence and purpose.

About The Author

Mort Greenberg brings over 25 years of experience as a business leader, working with tech start-ups and major media companies. Rising from an Account Executive to the President of a division with 800+ employees generating $220 million in annual revenue, Mort has supported revenue efforts for various companies as they navigated the need for growth, mergers, acquisitions, and IPOs. He was instrumental in shaping the digital advertising landscape during the early days of the Internet at Excite.com and Ask Jeeves. He has also held leadership roles at IAC / InterActiveCorp, NBC Universal, Nokia, and iHeartMedia. Along the way, he launched two companies of his own, FitAd and MindFlight, and learned that start-ups are not always successful. Since 2016, he has been helping turn around distressed media properties into profitable companies for a global private equity firm. The #1 lesson he has learned in all his years is that by improving people's revenue mindset, business problems are healed, and teams are motivated through innovation that new revenue affords.

www.ingramcontent.com/pod-product-compliance
Lightning Source LLC
Chambersburg PA
CBHW040900210326
41597CB00029B/4913